TRAVEL BUCKET LISTS

ARCHAEOLOGICAL SITE
BUCKET LIST

abdobooks.com

Published by Abdo Publishing, a division of ABDO, PO Box 398166, Minneapolis, Minnesota 55439. Copyright © 2022 by Abdo Consulting Group, Inc. International copyrights reserved in all countries. No part of this book may be reproduced in any form without written permission from the publisher. Core Library™ is a trademark and logo of Abdo Publishing.

Printed in the United States of America, North Mankato, Minnesota.
102021
012022

Cover Photo: Shutterstock Images
Interior Photos: Erik Harrison/Shutterstock Images, 4–5; Shutterstock Images, 9, 22, 40–41; iStockphoto, 12–13, 30, 34–35, 45; Red Line Editorial, 16, 24, 42–43; Daily Travel Photos/Shutterstock Images, 18–19; Cezary Wojtkowski/iStockphoto, 26–27; Mike Fuchslocher/Shutterstock Images, 32; Rafal Cichawa/Shutterstock Images, 38

Editor: Marie Pearson
Series Designer: Joshua Olson

Library of Congress Control Number: 2020948277

Publisher's Cataloging-in-Publication Data

Names: London, Martha, author.
Title: Archaeological site bucket list / by Martha London
Description: Minneapolis, Minnesota : Abdo Publishing, 2022 | Series: Travel bucket lists | Includes online resources and index
Identifiers: ISBN 9781532195235 (lib. bdg.) | ISBN 9781644947319 (pbk.) | ISBN 9781098215545 (ebook)
Subjects: LCSH: Travel--Juvenile literature. | Fertile Crescent--Juvenile literature. | Europe, Northern--Juvenile literature. | Asia--Juvenile literature. | Archaeological site location--Juvenile | Vacations--Juvenile literature.
Classification: DDC 910.20--dc23

CONTENTS

CHAPTER ONE

THE AMERICAS

The tourists slowly climbed the steep rock steps. Above them, the cliff formed a ceiling. The group was at Cliff Palace in Mesa Verde National Park in Colorado. Ancestral Puebloans built the structure approximately 1,400 years ago. They carved into the cliff face. They used stones and mortar to build up walls and create rooms.

The guide told the group that Cliff Palace had 150 rooms. Most cliff dwellings had fewer than five rooms. Researchers believe this was

Cliff Palace is the largest cliff dwelling in Mesa Verde National Park.

an important area. It may have been the center of trade and leadership for the Puebloans.

PERSPECTIVES

CHIMNEY ROCK

Chimney Rock is a site built by Ancestral Puebloans in what is now Colorado between 1025 and 1075 CE. Much of the stonework still exists. Researchers see evidence of a great house on the site. Stephen Lekson is a professor at the University of Colorado. He studies the ancient peoples of the southwestern United States. In an interview, he described how large great houses could be. He said, "Great Houses [are] monumental sandstone structures of up to 500 rooms, that rose up to five stories and covered over one hectare [2.5 acres] of area."

As the people walked through the rooms, they imagined living here. Extended family groups lived close to one another. They shared an open-air kiva. Kivas were gathering places. Families used the kivas for ceremonies.

The group climbed steep ladders to get to the next level on the cliff. Many of the smaller houses were broken. But some of the larger buildings were still standing. From far away, the buildings looked smooth. But up close, the people could see each individual stone.

The guide explained that scientists took samples of some of the plaster from inside the rooms. They analyzed the plaster. The scientists found that the plaster used to be brightly colored. Rooms were white, yellow, or red.

Cliff Palace is an archaeological site. People study archaeological sites using the science of archaeology. Scientists find objects from past civilizations. They may find written records of an area. But often no written records exist about the objects they find. Archaeologists frequently use artifacts to learn how people lived at different times and in different places.

Archaeologists study Cliff Palace to learn about the people who lived there in the late 1100s CE. Archaeological sites exist around the world. Some are more than 40,000 years old. Others are a few hundred years old. All of them hold clues to how people used to live.

TENOCHTITLÁN

There are several incredible archaeological sites throughout the Americas. Aztec cities were located in modern-day Mexico. In the mid-1300s CE, Aztec leaders created a central capital city, Tenochtitlán. It is located in what is now Mexico City. Excavations there help scientists piece together the daily lives of ancient Aztec people.

In 1345, Aztecs began building the

CHICHÉN ITZÁ

Chichén Itzá is an ancient Maya city in southern Mexico. The large city covers 4 square miles (10 sq km). Many of the larger buildings were constructed in approximately the 500s CE. One of these buildings is called the Castle. It is a large four-sided pyramid. The sides face north, south, east, and west. Each side has 91 steps. The top of the pyramid has an extra step. It has a total of 365 steps. This is equal to the number of days in the solar year.

Excavated ruins of Tenochtitlán are visible in Mexico City.

city on an island in Lake Texcoco. Over time, the city grew. Aztecs created human-made islands. People used canoes to travel between islands and to transport goods. Based on the size of the city, scientists believe between 200,000 and 400,000 people lived there.

Then Spanish forces took over the city in 1521. The Spanish destroyed many of the original artifacts. However, scientists can use written records from the Spanish army. These records help researchers understand the scale of the city. One record even noted the existence of a zoo.

MACHU PICCHU

One of the most famous archaeological sites of the Americas is Machu Picchu in present-day Peru. Machu Picchu was a mountaintop Inca city. It was built as early as the mid-1400s CE. The city was abandoned in the mid-1500s.

For hundreds of years, the site remained unknown to archaeologists. Until recently, it was only accessible by the Inca trail. Hiking to the site takes four to five days. However, once researchers took interest in the site, they were excited to begin studying it. They were willing to make the trek. Excavations began in 1912. Today people can take a train to see the ruins.

Due to the limited number of people who visited, much of the city remained intact. Flat, steplike areas called terraces on the mountainside were where the Inca farmed the land. Stonework allows scientists to see how the city was laid out. Today hundreds of thousands of tourists visit Machu Picchu each year.

STRAIGHT TO THE
SOURCE

Hiram Bingham is credited with sparking archaeological interest in Machu Picchu. Bingham studied the ruins in the 1910s and wrote about his findings:

> *We could make out a maze of ancient walls, the ruins of buildings made of blocks of granite, some of which were beautifully fitted together in the most refined style of Inca architecture. A few rods farther along we came to a little open space, on which were two splendid temples or palaces. The superior character of the stone work, the presence of these splendid edifices, and of what appeared to be an unusually large number of finely constructed stone dwellings, led me to believe that Machu Picchu might prove to be the largest and most important ruin discovered in South America since the days of the Spanish conquest.*

Source: Hiram Bingham. "In the Wonderland of Peru— Rediscovering Machu Picchu." *National Geographic*, nationalgeographic.com, 31 Mar. 2013. Accessed 24 June 2020.

CONSIDER YOUR AUDIENCE

Adapt this passage for a different audience, such as your younger friends. Write a blog post conveying this same information for the new audience. How does your post differ from the original text and why?

NORTHERN EUROPE

northern Europe includes, in part, the United Kingdom and the countries of Scandinavia. Some sites from the Neolithic period are in the United Kingdom. In northern Europe, the Neolithic period began in 7000 BCE. It lasted until 2300 BCE. Viking cities also exist in northern Europe. Scientists have found several in Sweden. Vikings lived from the 800s through the 1000s CE. Scientists look to these sites to learn about how people lived more than 1,000 years ago.

Stonehenge was built approximately 5,000 years ago in England.

PERSPECTIVES

RECONSTRUCTING A VILLAGE

West Stow in modern England was an Anglo-Saxon village between 420 and 650 CE. In the 1960s researchers worked to reconstruct what the village might have looked like. They used the same materials early villagers used. Ian Alister was one of the people who reconstructed the village. On the 40th anniversary of the village, Alister said, "It's very satisfying that the thing has survived, because a lot of people . . . thought the huts would blow down in the first [storm]."

STONEHENGE

Stonehenge is a circle of megaliths on Salisbury Plain in England. Megaliths are large stones set next to other stones to form a monument. Scientists are still puzzled as to how the Neolithic peoples constructed the site. But scientists do have a good idea of when the site was built.

Researchers tested the stones. They took photos from the air. Mounds show outlines where previous stones stood. Testing shows the site was built in stages. Researchers found human remains nearby from 3030 BCE. This was approximately the time ancient people made a circular structure of dirt, long before the iconic stones were placed. Neolithic peoples began placing stones sometime between 2400 and 2200 BCE.

Scientists continue to study the site. It was once a cemetery and a religious site. But many mysteries remain.

BIRKA

Birka was a Viking-age town in southeastern Sweden. Vikings were Scandinavian warriors. They were expert sailors. Vikings eventually colonized large areas of Europe and traveled to North America.

THE STANDING STONES

Stonehenge is not the only human-made circle of stones. The Stones of Stenness are on the Orkney Islands in Scotland. The formation was originally a circle of 12 stones. Four stones remain. Some of the stones are 20 feet (6 m) tall. The floor of a fireplace is at the center of the circle. Scientists are not certain what the Stones of Stenness were used for. Recent studies suggest they were used to study stars.

VIKINGS ACROSS THE SEA

This map shows the sailing routes of Vikings from the 800s to the 1000s CE. How does this map help you better understand the text?

Birka was built in the mid-700s CE. Excavations revealed Birka was an important trading port. At the time, it was the closest port to eastern Europe. Vikings traded with the peoples in eastern Europe and western Asia. The city had many craftspeople. Weavers worked with wool. Blacksmiths made iron tools. Some people used horns to make combs. The people of Birka traded these objects with other regions. Artifacts from around the world were found in the city, including fabric, glass, and ceramic pieces. Archaeologists also found silver coins from the Middle East. Additionally, excavations revealed many weapons. It was likely people needed to defend themselves from pirates.

But after 200 years, the city was abandoned. Scientists are not entirely sure why. It may have been because sea levels dropped. As a result, Birka was no longer on the coast. It could not bring ships to port. A new trading center was created.

EXPLORE ONLINE

Chapter Two discusses Stonehenge. The website below explores religious beliefs at the time Stonehenge was made and how architecture played a role. As you know, every source is different. How is the information from the website the same as the information in Chapter Two? What new information did you learn from the website?

STONE AGE BELIEFS

abdocorelibrary.com/archaeological-site-bucket-list

THE FERTILE CRESCENT AND BEYOND

The Fertile Crescent has been called the birthplace of civilization. The area includes parts of what are now Egypt, Israel, Iraq, Jordan, Syria, and Iran. Ancient peoples lived near the rivers that flow through the lands. The yearly flooding made the soil fertile. People grew crops. Ancient civilizations thrived. Cities and empires continued for thousands of years. The Fertile Crescent and regions extending into southern Europe have always been culturally diverse.

Scientists are still unsure exactly how the ancient Egyptians built the Pyramids of Giza.

Today these areas are divided into many countries. But thousands of years ago, the borders were different.

PERSPECTIVES

EGYPTIAN AFTERLIFE

Egyptian people believed in life after death. Many Egyptians were mummified when they died. Their bodies were carefully preserved for use in the afterlife. The most famous mummies are those of the ancient kings. Salima Ikram is an Egyptologist. She is one of the scientists who studies mummies. In an interview, she explained that mummies hold clues to life in ancient Egypt. She said, "There's also a lot that we can learn from mummies about ancient disease, medical practices, technology, health, diet, as well as religious beliefs."

Empires crossed over oceans and large areas of land. Some regions were connected through political and military rule.

THE PYRAMIDS OF GIZA

Ancient Egyptians built many pyramids. The largest are the three pyramids at Giza, Egypt. These pyramids were built between 2575 and 2465 BCE. Each was a tomb for a king. The pyramids are named after the kings who were buried in them. They are Khufu, Khafre, and Menkaure.

The Khufu and Khafre pyramids were originally more than 450 feet (170 m) tall. The Menkaure pyramid was originally 218 feet (66 m) tall. Egyptian kings were buried with gold and other valuable artifacts. These objects were for the kings in the afterlife.

People looted the pyramids in ancient times. The items that were once in the pyramids are gone. Today the pyramids are protected. Scientists study them. Paintings and written works help scientists learn how people lived in ancient Egypt.

PERSEPOLIS

Persepolis was the large capital city of the Persian empire. The ruins of Persepolis are in modern-day Iran. Archaeologists study how the buildings were constructed. They look at the ruins. Scientists learn about early building techniques. Construction of the city began in 518 BCE.

The ruins of Persepolis include many beautiful carvings.

Archaeologists found pestles in Persepolis. Pestles are stone or metal tools used to grind small amounts of grain or spices. They also found other tools such as needles. The site has many ceramic jars.

Written texts were also found at Persepolis. These texts included details about sales. For example, one text lists a payment of barley for a worker. These items paint an important picture for archaeologists. Researchers can piece together what items people bought and sold. As a result, they begin to understand what a typical day in the Persepolis economy looked like.

ACROPOLIS

The Acropolis in Athens, Greece, was built in the 400s BCE. Many impressive ruins remain today. Athena was the city's main goddess.

A huge temple to Athena was built at the center of the Acropolis. Large columns surround the temple. Archaeologists study texts written about how the Acropolis was built. Records show it took two years of planning before construction began on the temple.

AQUEDUCTS

Civilizations around the world have used aqueducts. These structures bring fresh water to a city or farm. Some of the most famous aqueducts were built by the Roman Empire. Roman builders used arches for some of the aqueducts. Arches allowed aqueducts to cross valleys. Some of the aqueducts are still used in modern Rome. One brings water to a city fountain.

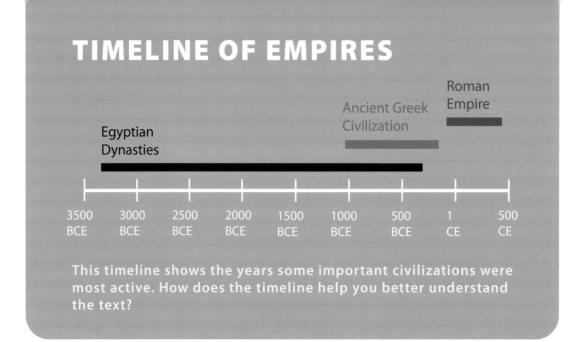

TIMELINE OF EMPIRES

Roman
Empire

Ancient Greek
Civilization

Egyptian
Dynasties

| 3500 BCE | 3000 BCE | 2500 BCE | 2000 BCE | 1500 BCE | 1000 BCE | 500 BCE | 1 CE | 500 CE |

This timeline shows the years some important civilizations were most active. How does the timeline help you better understand the text?

Hundreds of people were involved. Stonemasons, painters, and sculptors all worked on the project.

The Acropolis was a place for people to bring gifts and requests to Athena. Yearly celebrations brought many people to Athens. They visited the huge statue of Athena in the temple. The statue was made of ivory and gold.

THE COLOSSEUM

The Colosseum opened in 80 CE. This amphitheater in Rome, Italy, was used for 400 years. People gathered in the stadium. They watched games, fights, and races. It could even be flooded for ship battles.

The Colosseum was one of the first freestanding amphitheaters. Most had to be built into the side of a hill. Without support, earlier amphitheaters sometimes collapsed. Rome's Colosseum was built for large public gatherings. The stadium could fit 50,000 people. Archaeologists see evidence of public bathrooms and even drinking fountains.

FURTHER EVIDENCE

Chapter Three has information about ancient civilizations in the Fertile Crescent. What is the main point of this chapter? What key evidence supports this point? Go to the article about the Fertile Crescent at the website below. Find a quote from the website that supports the chapter's main point.

WHERE IS THE FERTILE CRESCENT?

abdocorelibrary.com/archaeological-site-bucket-list

ASIA

sia is the largest continent on Earth. Many ruins of ancient civilizations exist there. Huge cities have dotted the landscape for thousands of years. Archaeologists look at these sites for clues to how ancient cities worked. They also look for information on how civilizations traded with one another across large distances.

Some ancient buildings throughout Asia contain images of a religious figure named the Buddha.

RAKHIGARHI

The Indus civilization was massive. It covered 386,000 square miles (1 million sq km) from approximately 2500 to 1700 BCE. The Indus civilization spread throughout what is now Pakistan and into northwestern India. Researchers compare the importance of the Indus civilization to that of ancient Egypt. The largest city of the Indus civilization was Rakhigarhi. The city is located in present-day India.

Archaeologists rediscovered

PERSPECTIVES
THE SILK ROAD

The Silk Road was a series of trade routes. The routes connected China with the Middle East and Europe. Traders used the Silk Road from 130 BCE to 1453 CE. People traded spices, fabric, and other goods along the route. Researchers used written records to piece together the route. They found the locations of trading posts. Marco Polo was famous for documenting his travels along the Silk Road. He traveled it in the 1200s. He wrote a book called *The Travels of Marco Polo*, describing his experiences in China.

Rakhigarhi in 1920. They also excavated parts of the city in the 1960s and 2000s. Scientists studied building ruins. Archaeologists reconstructed how parts of the city were laid out. Scientists also found many small objects within the buildings. They found clay toys that resembled pigs. There were burnt clay pots. There were pieces from an ancient furnace. The furnace showed that part of the city was industrial.

TERRACOTTA ARMY

Farther east is one of the largest burial sites in the world. It is the grave of China's first emperor, Qin Shi Huang. Qin took the throne in 221 BCE. He unified several areas

KOREKAWA

People of prehistoric Japan were part of the Jōmon culture. This culture began as early as 10,500 BCE and lasted until 300 BCE. Jōmon people created beautiful and complex pottery. Several Jōmon sites exist across Japan. One of these is Korekawa in the northeastern part of the island of Honshu. Korekawa was a small but bustling village. Excavations reveal separate areas for housing, a cemetery, and a dump for waste.

Each terracotta soldier has a unique face and hairstyle.

of China. According to written documents, the emperor ordered workers to begin building his mausoleum in the first few years of his reign. A mausoleum is a large burial building for a person who has died. Construction continued even after his death in 210 BCE. The mausoleum contains thousands of terracotta soldiers. Terracotta is a type of clay. The clay army and other objects, including bronze horses and wooden chariots, were sealed in with the emperor. They were meant to protect him in the afterlife.

The first soldier was found in 1974. Since then scientists have found thousands more clay soldiers and artifacts. Scientists continue to find more objects. Some archaeologists say the total number of clay soldiers might never be known.

The terracotta army is a small part of Qin's mausoleum. Inside the mausoleum is Qin's tomb. Scientists found high levels of mercury in the mausoleum. Mercury is a poisonous heavy metal. These findings match ancient texts. These texts describe how the mausoleum had mercury rivers to keep people from disturbing the tomb.

ANGKOR WAT

Angkor Wat is a large temple in Cambodia. It was built at the beginning of the 1100s as a Hindu temple. It was so big that it was also the kingdom's capital city.

Angkor Wat is an important cultural and religious site.

At the end of the 1100s, Hindu leaders lost control of the temple. Angkor Wat turned into a Buddhist temple. Buddhist monks used the temple into the 1800s. Its size made it difficult to care for. Over time, as fewer monks lived there, the temple was damaged. Trees and plants began to grow over the stones. Earthquakes damaged the temple. In the 1900s, scientific groups began to repair and restore the temple. Today tourists visit the site.

STRAIGHT TO THE
SOURCE

Sima Qian was a historian in China in the early 100s BCE. In one text, he wrote of Qin's mausoleum:

More than 700,000 convict laborers from the world were sent there. They dug through three springs, poured in liquid bronze, and secured the sarcophagus [coffin]. Houses, officials, unusual and valuable things were moved in to fill it. [Qin] ordered artisans to make crossbows triggered by mechanisms. Anyone passing before them would be shot immediately. They used mercury to create rivers, the Jiang and the He, and the great seas, wherein the mercury was circulated mechanically. On the ceiling were celestial bodies and on the ground geographical features.

Source: Mark Cartwright. "Terracotta Army." *Ancient History Encyclopedia*, 6 Nov. 2017, ancient.eu. Accessed 25 June 2020.

BACK IT UP

The author of this passage is using evidence to support a point. Write a paragraph describing the point the author is making. Then write down two or three pieces of evidence the author uses to make the point.

AFRICA

The Fertile Crescent may have been the birthplace of modern civilization, but Africa was the birthplace of modern humans. The oldest human and prehuman remains were found in Africa. Rich in natural resources, ancient African civilizations traded with one another. They also provided resources for ancient civilizations around the world.

Kilwa includes the ruins of ancient mosques.

LAAS GEEL

Laas Geel is a collection of cave paintings in present-day Somalia. Researchers believe the paintings are 4,000 to 5,000 years old. This makes them the oldest cave paintings in northeast Africa. The paintings of Laas Geel are in a series of connected caves. Paintings include images of cattle and humans. The art was sheltered from weather. Researchers can identify different colors of paints people used.

KILWA

Kilwa was an island city-state off the coast of present-day Tanzania. A city-state is a city that governs itself and the surrounding area. Kilwa was founded in the 800s CE. Swahili and Muslim traders worked in the city. The city soon became a trading center for gold and enslaved people from the African interior. This slave trade was first run by people from what is now the Middle East.

The rich trading allowed the city to grow. Based on its size, archaeologists believe at least 10,000 people lived in the city. Traders were unable to grow their own food on the island. They got food from the Bantu peoples on the Swahili Coast of Africa.

Scientists study the ruins of the city. The palace, the mosque, and many stone buildings remain. Archaeologists believe the artistic details show Kilwa was a city with many wealthy merchants.

Kilwa had a good location. Its traders could sail to India, China, and nations on the Persian Gulf. Further excavations revealed that people

PERSPECTIVES
PROTECTING THE NOK FIGURES

The Nok people lived in what is now Nigeria. Researchers believe the Nok culture may have been the earliest civilization in West Africa. The Nok culture was active from approximately 500 BCE to 200 CE. Sites associated with Nok culture had beautiful terracotta statues and iron furnaces. Peter Breunig is a professor in Germany. He explained that many artifacts were lost because scientists did not work to protect the site right away. He said, "Instead of scientific exploration, the Nok became a victim of illegal digging and international art dealers."

Scientists had to excavate the Gedi ruins from the surrounding forest.

in Kilwa also made cotton cloth. Traders mined or purchased ivory, glass, and copper to produce trading goods.

GEDI RUINS

The Gedi ruins are located in what is now Kenya. Founded in approximately the 1100s CE, Gedi was a large coastal city. The city was surrounded by two walls. Scientists uncovered the walls during excavations. The two walls give scientists a clearer idea of how the city was run. They believe there was likely a clear economic class system. The rich lived within the inner wall.

Politicians, royalty, and wealthy merchants could afford to build stone houses. Farmers and peasants lived between the inner and outer walls. These people most likely lived in mud huts.

Several ruins within the inner wall give scientists a clue to the past. Some of the buildings had no windows. Researchers believe the rich stored gold and jewels in these buildings. Rooms were only accessible by climbing through a door on the roof.

The city was abandoned in the 1600s. Researchers are not yet sure why. But they believe it may be one of two reasons. The first is that the wells could have dried up. Without water, the people would have had to leave. The other reason may be that Portuguese colonizers forced people in Gedi to leave.

GREAT ZIMBABWE

The Shona people lived in the city known as Great Zimbabwe between 1100 and 1400 CE. The large city in what is now the nation of Zimbabwe covered more than

High walls surround the Great Enclosure in Great Zimbabwe. The Valley Ruins lie below it.

200 acres (80 ha). Researchers believe between 10,000 and 20,000 people lived in the city. Great Zimbabwe is known for the complicated stonework on the buildings.

The Shona were farmers. They grew crops and raised cattle. The Shona people also exported gold to traders at ports such as Kilwa.

Archaeologists continue to study the area. They discovered three main sections to the city. Each section served a specific purpose. At the top of the hill are the oldest structures. Scientists believe this area was

used for religious ceremonies. The Great Enclosure is a section named for its large stone wall. The wall creates a large circle. Below the Enclosure are the Valley Ruins. Scientists found stone houses. They believe this is where most of the people lived.

There are incredible archaeological sites all over the world. Scientists study the sites to learn how people in the past lived. Tourists visit these sites to see the amazing structures and walk where other people lived hundreds or thousands of years ago.

N
W · E
S

Pacific Ocean

Atlantic Ocean

1 Cliff Palace (Colorado)

2 Tenochtitlán (Mexico)

3 Machu Picchu (Peru)

4 Stonehenge
(United Kingdom)

5 Birka (Sweden)

6 Colosseum (Italy)

7 Acropolis (Greece)

8 Pyramids of Giza (Egypt)

9 Gedi ruins (Kenya)

10 Kilwa (Tanzania)

11 Great Zimbabwe
(Zimbabwe)

12 Persepolis (Iran)

13 Rakhigarhi (India)

14 Qin Shi Huang's
mausoleum (China)

15 Angkor Wat (Cambodia)

Arctic Ocean

Indian Ocean

Southern Ocean

Tell the Tale

Chapter One of this book discusses a group exploring and learning about Ancestral Puebloan culture at Cliff Palace. Imagine you are on a similar trip. Write 200 words about the architecture and artifacts you see.

Dig Deeper

After reading this book, what questions do you still have about archaeological sites? With an adult's help, find a few reliable sources that can help you answer your questions. Write a paragraph about what you learned.

Say What?

Studying archaeological sites can mean learning a lot of new vocabulary. Find five words in this book you've never heard before. Use a dictionary to find out what they mean. Then write the meanings in your own words and use each word in a new sentence.

You Are There

This book discusses several archaeological sites from around the world. Imagine you are exploring one of them. Write a letter home telling your friends what you have found. What do you notice about the site? Be sure to add plenty of detail to your notes.

GLOSSARY

amphitheater
an oval outdoor stadium

ceramic
having to do with a material such as clay that has been shaped and hardened by heating it

colonized
settled by people from another country

economic class
a division based on how much money or property a person has

excavation
the uncovering of layers of soil to reveal objects from the past

export
to sell a product to another region

fertile
good for growing crops

industrial
having to do with the production of goods

loot
to illegally remove archaeological artifacts

mortar
a substance used to hold stones together in a building

ONLINE RESOURCES

To learn more about archaeological sites, visit our free resource websites below.

Visit **abdocorelibrary.com** or scan this QR code for free Common Core resources for teachers and students, including vetted activities, multimedia, and booklinks, for deeper subject comprehension.

Visit **abdobooklinks.com** or scan this QR code for free additional online weblinks for further learning. These links are routinely monitored and updated to provide the most current information available.

LEARN MORE

Alkire, Jessie. *Exploring Ancient Cities*. Abdo Publishing, 2019.

Hamilton, John. *Colorado*. Abdo Publishing, 2017.

LaPierre, Yvette. *Engineering the Colosseum*. Abdo Publishing, 2018.

INDEX

About the Author

Martha London is a writer and educator. She lives in Minnesota and hopes to one day take a trip (or trips!) to all of these locations.